Tarantulas

by Conrad J. Storad
photographs by Paula Jansen

Lerner Publications Company • Minneapolis, Minnesota

For my sister, Carolyn, and my brothers, Michael, James, David, and Joseph. You are the very best!
—CJS

To my sisters and brother, Ginny, Nancy, Christy, and Ed, with whom I've enjoyed many wonders of the world.
—PJ

The photographer extends special thanks to Deborah Thirkhill, Education Keeper, Phoenix Zoo; Renee Lizotte and the Arizona-Sonora Desert Museum; and The Pet Pad, Tempe, Arizona.

Photographs on pages 30 and 36 are © Robert & Linda Mitchell.

Thanks to our series consultant, Sharyn Fenwick, elementary science/math specialist. Mrs. Fenwick was the winner of the National Science Teachers Association 1991 Distinguished Teaching Award. She also was the recipient of the Presidential Award for Excellence in Math and Science Teaching, representing the state of Minnesota at the elementary level in 1992.

Early Bird Nature Books were conceptualized by Ruth Berman and designed by Steve Foley. Series editor is Joelle Goldman.

Library of Congress Cataloging-in-Publication Data

Storad, Conrad J.
    Tarantulas / Conrad J. Storad ; photographs by Paula Jansen.
        p.   cm. — (Early bird nature books)
    Includes index.
    Summary: Describes the physical characteristics, behavior, enemies, and habitats of the biggest and hairiest spiders.
    ISBN 0-8225-3024-4 (alk. paper)
    1. Tarantulas—Juvenile literature. [1. Tarantulas.]
I. Jansen, Paula, ill. II. Title. III. Series.
QL458.42.T5S88   1998
595.4'4—dc21   97-5141

Manufactured in the United States of America
1 2 3 4 5 6 – SP – 03 02 01 00 99 98

Contents

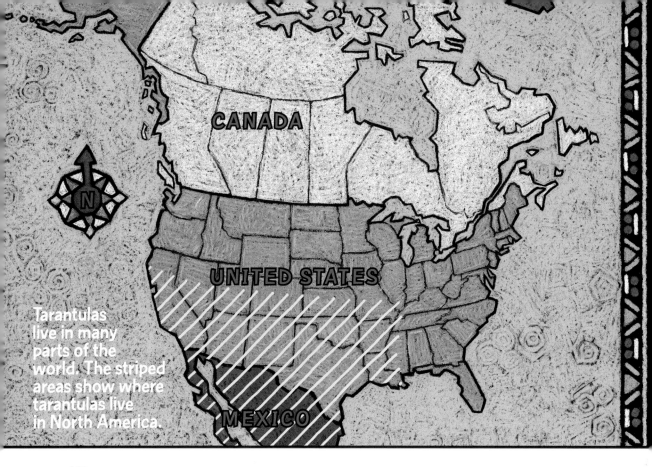

Tarantulas live in many parts of the world. The striped areas show where tarantulas live in North America.

Be a Word Detective

Can you find these words as you read about the tarantula's life? Be a detective and try to figure out what they mean. You can turn to the glossary on page 46 for help.

abdomen	**fangs**	**prey**
arachnids	**molting**	**prosoma**
arboreal	**nocturnal**	**spiderlings**
egg sac	**predators**	**venom**
exoskeleton		

Chapter 1

Tarantulas are spiders. How many eyes do most spiders have?

Spiders, Spiders Everywhere

Spiders are scary-looking creatures. Up close, they look like monsters from outer space. Spiders have fangs and eight legs. Most spiders have eight eyes.

But spiders are not from outer space. They live on Earth. Spiders have lived here for hundreds of millions of years.

Spiders belong to a group of animals called arachnids (uh-RACK-nidz). Scorpions, ticks, and mites are also arachnids.

Spiders come in all sizes, shapes, and colors. Some spiders are smaller than the head of a pin. Others are much larger. Scientists call the biggest, hairiest spiders theraphosids (ther-uh-FOH-sidz). Most people call these spiders tarantulas (tuh-RAN-chuh-luhz).

Scorpions are related to spiders. All scorpions and spiders have eight legs.

About 30 kinds of tarantulas live in the United States. Most of them live in the deserts and pine forests of Arizona, Texas, New Mexico, and southern California.

Scientists have found over 700 kinds of tarantulas. Most tarantulas live in wet jungles. Others live in deserts. All tarantulas are nocturnal. That means they are active at night.

Many people keep Mexican red knee tarantulas as pets.

Tarantulas have odd names. The names explain where the tarantulas live and what they look like. There are tarantulas named the Mexican red knee, the Chilean yellow rump, and the South American pink toe.

The largest tarantulas are called bird-eating spiders.
The scientific name of the Goliath bird-eating spider
is Theraphosa leblondi.

The biggest spider of all is the Goliath bird-eating spider. This tarantula lives in jungles in South America. Most tarantulas weigh about 1 ounce. A Goliath weighs up to 4 ounces. That is as heavy as a chicken's egg. A Goliath is much bigger than your open hand. The bodies of some Goliaths are 3 inches across. From leg tip to leg tip, these spiders measure up to 10 inches. That is as wide as your dinner plate!

Many people are afraid of spiders. Even more people are afraid of tarantulas, because tarantulas are big and hairy. But people should not be afraid of tarantulas. They are shy creatures. Tarantulas spend most of their lives hiding.

Most tarantulas don't bite people unless people frighten them.

Chapter 2

Deserts are often hot during the day and cool at night. When do desert tarantulas hunt for food?

Burrows and Webs

 Jungle tarantulas need moist air. If the air is not wet enough, these spiders dry up and die. Desert tarantulas are tougher. They hide in cool places during the day. Cool places keep these tarantulas from drying up. At night, the desert is cooler. Then the tarantulas come out to hunt for food.

All spiders can make silk with their bodies. Some spiders use silk to make webs. But most tarantulas do not spin webs. They dig holes in the ground to live in. The holes are called burrows. Tarantulas line their burrows with silk.

A tarantula uses its jaws to dig its burrow. Desert tarantulas dig deep burrows to reach cool sand.

Tarantulas do not need much space. Most tarantulas dig small, tight burrows. As the spider grows, it makes its burrow larger. Sometimes a tarantula leaves when its burrow becomes too small. It digs a new burrow in a different spot.

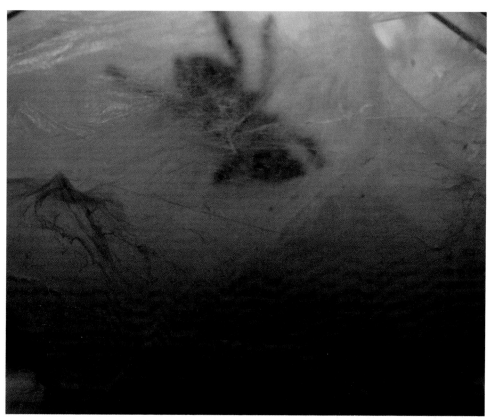

All spiders can make silk. Some tarantulas use silk to make their homes.

A tarantula is hiding in its tube web.

Some jungle tarantulas live high in the trees. These spiders are called arboreal (ar-BOR-ee-uhl) tarantulas. Arboreal means "living in the trees." Arboreal tarantulas spin webs that are shaped like tubes. Tube webs are not thin like the spider webs you might find in your basement. Tube webs have thick walls.

Chapter 3

Tarantulas are hunters. What creatures do tarantulas hunt?

The Hunter and the Hunted

Tarantulas are predators (PREH-duh-turz). They hunt other animals for food. The animals they hunt are called prey. A tarantula's prey includes crickets, cockroaches, beetles, moths, and other insects.

Even the tarantulas who are called bird eaters usually eat insects. But sometimes baby birds fall out of their nests in the jungle. Giant tarantulas may gobble up these babies. Tiny mice may wander near a tarantula's tube web. They become supper for the spider.

This tarantula has caught a cricket.

Most spiders do not need good eyes to catch food. Their sticky webs catch insects for them. When a trapped insect tries to get away, it shakes the web. The shaking helps the spider find the insect.

Many spiders use sticky webs to catch insects. But a tarantula runs out and grabs insects that come near its home.

A tarantula has eight eyes. But it cannot see well. If objects are more than a few feet away, the tarantula cannot tell what they are.

Tarantulas do not spin webs to trap insects. They use their eyes to look for food. Most tarantulas have two large eyes. Around the large eyes are up to six smaller eyes.

A tarantula's fangs are just below its eyes.

All spiders have fangs. Fangs are long,
sharp, hollow teeth. Most spiders' fangs move
from side to side, like scissors. But a tarantula's
fangs strike downward, like two big hooks.

A tarantula uses its fangs for biting. The fangs hold a poison called venom. Tarantulas use venom to kill the insects they eat.

Most tarantulas' venom is too weak to kill a human. But some kinds of tarantulas have powerful venom. People have died from the bite of these spiders.

The sharp tips of a tarantula's fangs are usually hidden under its body.

Tarantulas are clever hunters. A tarantula sits quietly just inside the door to its burrow. It waits for prey to come near. Then the tarantula runs out of its burrow. It uses its front legs to grab the prey. The tarantula's jaws slam down. Its fangs inject venom into the prey. The venom keeps the prey from moving.

When a tarantula is ready to attack, it rears up on its back legs.

A tarantula may finish eating in 20 minutes. Or the spider may take several hours to finish its meal.

Sometimes a tarantula wraps its catch in silk. The tarantula drags the food inside its burrow and saves it for later. When suppertime arrives, the tarantula uses its jaws to break the insect into pieces. Then the spider spits strong juices onto the pieces. These juices melt parts of the insect into mushy goop. The spider sucks up the goop. All that remains is a pile of hard bits that the spider cannot drink.

The hard parts of a cricket are on the ground near this tarantula. They are all that is left of the spider's meal.

Crickets and moths have soft bodies. They are easy for spiders to eat. But beetles have tough shells. It is hard for a tarantula to break a beetle into pieces. Instead, a tarantula uses its fangs to poke holes through a beetle's shell. The spider pours juices through the holes. The juices melt the beetle's insides. The tarantula sucks out the gooey soup. Then the spider throws away the shell, as if it were an empty milk carton.

Most adult tarantulas eat only about once a week. But the larger tarantulas are always hungry. A 4-ounce Goliath can eat 4 ounces of insects every day. That's a lot of bugs!

Tarantulas can live for months without eating, but they always need water. Desert tarantulas get water from the insects they eat. They also drink dew from plants and rocks.

Tarantulas can live for a long time without food. But they always need fresh water to drink.

Chapter 4

A tarantula's body has two main parts. What are the parts called?

Hairy, Scary Body Parts

A tarantula's body has two main parts. The parts are the prosoma (proh-SOH-muh) and the abdomen (AB-duh-muhn). A narrow waist connects the prosoma and the abdomen. The waist is called the pedicel (PEH-duh-sehl).

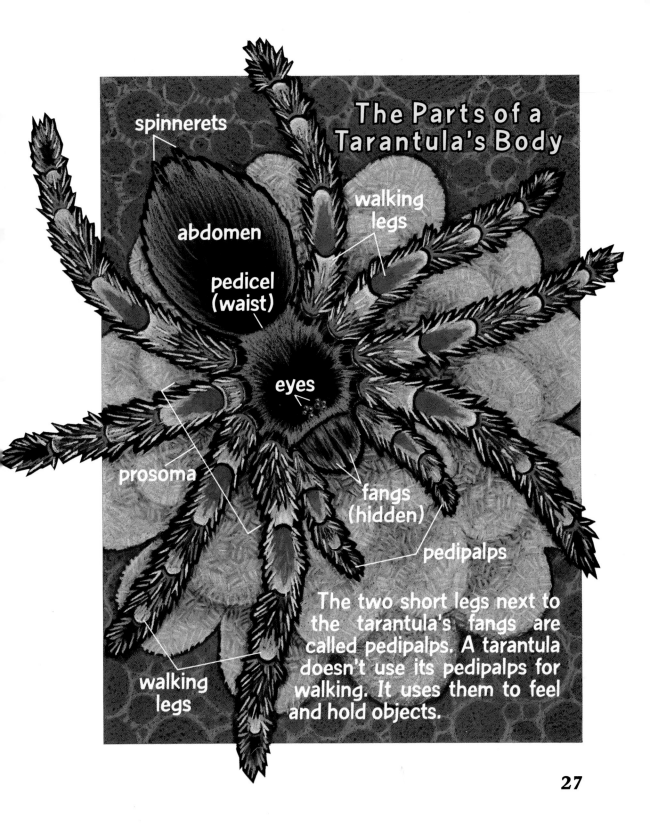

The Parts of a Tarantula's Body

spinnerets

abdomen

pedicel (waist)

walking legs

eyes

prosoma

fangs (hidden)

pedipalps

walking legs

The two short legs next to the tarantula's fangs are called pedipalps. A tarantula doesn't use its pedipalps for walking. It uses them to feel and hold objects.

This display in a museum shows the tracks a tarantula makes when it walks. The four legs on each side of a tarantula's body touch the ground near one another.

The prosoma is the front part of a spider's body. It includes the head, eyes, jaws, and fangs. The eight walking legs are attached to the bottom of the prosoma.

The abdomen is the big, round part of a spider's body. The spider's heart and lungs are in the abdomen. At the very back of the abdomen are the spinnerets. The spinnerets make threads of silk.

A tarantula's abdomen is weak. If a tarantula falls even a short distance, its abdomen may split open. Then the tarantula will bleed to death.

A tarantula has no bones. Its skin is its skeleton. The tarantula's skin is called an exoskeleton (ek-soh-SKEL-uh-tuhn), which means "outside skeleton." The exoskeleton is hard. It does not stretch.

As a tarantula grows, it must shed its skin. The shedding of old skin is called molting. It takes about three hours for a tarantula to molt.

Tarantulas molt while lying on their backs. This tarantula is pulling its legs out of its old skin. The spider's new skin is darker than the old skin.

A tarantula left behind this empty skin.

Tarantulas who live on the ground usually molt out in the open. Arboreal tarantulas molt inside their tube webs.

When a tarantula molts, a new, larger skin replaces the old one. It takes time for the new skin to harden. While the new skin is still soft, the tarantula cannot walk.

A tarantula's body and legs are covered with long hairs.

The hairs on a tarantula's body help it to feel tiny movements. When animals move, the ground or tree leaves shake. A tarantula can feel the shaking. It can tell when another creature is near.

Some of a tarantula's hairs are tiny stingers. These hairs protect the tarantula from its enemies. When a tarantula is afraid, it scratches its body hard with a back leg. This scratching launches many stinging hairs into the air. The hairs hurt lizards, snakes, birds, and other spiders. The sting keeps these animals from bothering the tarantula.

This tarantula has kicked many stinging hairs at its enemies. Now it has a bald spot on its abdomen. The hairs will grow back the next time the spider molts.

Chapter 5

*Baby tarantulas
hatch from eggs.
How many eggs does
a mother tarantula
lay at one time?*

From Egg to Adult

Baby tarantulas are called spiderlings. Spiderlings hatch from eggs. When a female tarantula is ready to lay eggs, she makes a bag out of silk. The bag is called an egg sac. It

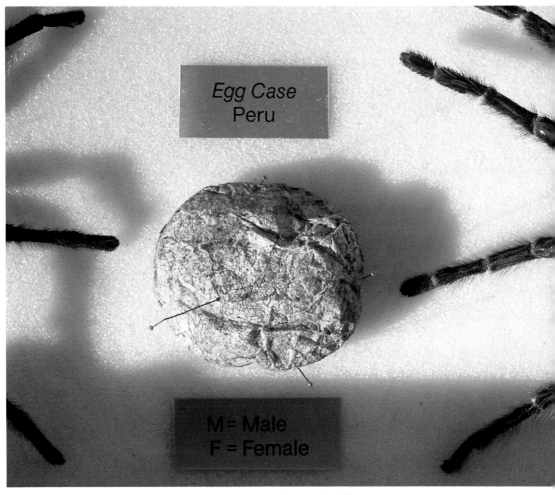

A female tarantula lays her eggs on a sheet of silk.
She wraps the silk around the eggs to make her egg sac.

looks like a golf ball made out of cotton. The
tarantula lays as many as 700 eggs inside the
egg sac. She stays near her eggs. She may stop
eating until the spiderlings have hatched.

These newly hatched tarantulas are still inside their egg sac.

A tarantula's eggs hatch 3 to 16 weeks after they are laid. The newly hatched spiderlings look nothing like mom or dad. They look like tiny white eggs with legs. After hatching, each spiderling digs its own burrow. The spiderlings grow inside their burrows.

Tarantula spiderlings molt for the first time while they are still inside the egg sac. They molt again when they are about a week old. The baby tarantulas begin hunting for food after their second molt. Spiderlings eat baby crickets, fruit flies, and other small insects.

Baby tarantulas molt several times each year. After they are two years old, they molt only once or twice each year.

An arboreal tarantula makes her egg sac inside her tube web. After her spiderlings hatch, they stay in the tube web for several days. They eat insects that their mother catches. Once they leave, the spiderlings must build their own webs.

As a young tarantula grows up, it looks more and more like its parents.

Most tarantulas who live in the United States take 10 to 12 years to become adults.

Growing up takes 2 to 12 years for a tarantula. Male tarantulas live for only one or two years after they are grown. Females live longer. Wild female tarantulas can live 12 to 14 years after they are grown. Females who are pets may live to be 30 years old.

Chapter 6

If an enemy grabs a tarantula's leg, the leg may break off. Then the spider runs away. The leg will grow back the next time the spider molts. What animals eat tarantulas?

Spider Hunters

Tarantulas are good hunters. But they are also food for other predators. They are tasty treats for owls, hawks, coyotes, weasels, snakes, lizards, and large scorpions.

Molting is a dangerous time for tarantulas. When a tarantula molts, it may lie on its back out in the open for several hours. It must wait while its new skin hardens. It cannot run away. It is an easy meal for a predator.

Owls and other large birds hunt tarantulas.

The tarantula hawk wasp is the tarantula's worst enemy. These wasps are not afraid of tarantulas. A wasp crawls into a tarantula's burrow, and a fight begins. If the tarantula wins, it eats the wasp. If the wasp wins, it stings the tarantula. The wasp's venom does not kill the tarantula. But the spider will never move again.

When a tarantula hawk wasp attacks a tarantula, the spider rears up to bite it with its fangs. Then the wasp stings the tarantula under its abdomen.

Tarantulas need places to live. When people move into the deserts and rain forests, there is less room for tarantulas.

After it stings the tarantula, the wasp lays an egg on the tarantula's body. A few weeks later, the egg hatches. The baby wasp does not have to hunt for food. It has a live spider to eat.

Life in the wild is hard for all creatures. They struggle to find food and to avoid being eaten. Tarantulas and other spiders have done well at both jobs. That is why spiders have survived for millions of years.

On Sharing a Book

As you know, adults greatly influence a child's attitude toward reading. When a child sees you read, or when you share a book with a child, you're sending a message that reading is important. Show the child that reading a book together is important to you. Find a comfortable, quiet place. Turn off the television and limit other distractions, such as telephone calls.

Be prepared to start slowly. Take turns reading parts of this book. Stop and talk about what you're reading. Talk about the photographs. You may find that much of the shared time is spent discussing just a few pages. This discussion time is valuable for both of you, so don't move through the book too quickly. If the child begins to lose interest, stop reading. Continue sharing the book at another time. When you do pick up the book again, be sure to revisit the parts you have already read. Most importantly, enjoy the book!

Be a Vocabulary Detective

You will find a word list on page 5. Words selected for this list are important to the understanding of the topic of this book. Encourage the child to be a word detective and search for the words as you read the book together. Talk about what the words mean and how they are used in the sentence. Do any of these words have more than one meaning? You will find these words defined in a glossary on page 46.

What about Questions?

Use questions to make sure the child understands the information in this book. Here are some suggestions:

What did this paragraph tell us? What does this picture show? What do you think we'll learn about next? Could a tarantula live in your backyard? Why/Why not? How do tarantulas get their food? How do they eat? Why must a tarantula shed its skin as it grows? How does a tarantula defend itself? How long does it take for a tarantula to grow up? What do you think it's like being a tarantula? What is your favorite part of the book? Why?

If the child has questions, don't hesitate to respond with questions of your own, such as: What do *you* think? Why? What is it that you don't know? If the child can't remember certain facts, turn to the index.

Introducing the Index

The index is an important learning tool. It helps readers get information quickly without searching throughout the whole book. Turn to the index on page 47. Choose an entry, such as *eyes,* and ask the child to use the index to find out how many eyes a tarantula has. Repeat this exercise with as many entries as you like. Ask the child to point out the differences between an index and a glossary. (The index helps readers find information quickly, while the glossary tells readers what words mean.)

Where in the World?

Many plants and animals found in the Early Bird Nature Books series live in parts of the world other than the United States. Encourage the child to find the places mentioned in this book on a world map or globe. Take time to talk about climate, terrain, and how you might live in such places.

All the World in Metric!

Although our monetary system is in metric units (based on multiples of 10), the United States is one of the few countries in the world that does not use the metric system of measurement. Here are some conversion activities you and the child can do using a calculator:

WHEN YOU KNOW:	MULTIPLY BY:	TO FIND:
miles	1.609	kilometers
feet	0.3048	meters
inches	2.54	centimeters
gallons	3.787	liters
tons	0.907	metric tons
pounds	0.454	kilograms

Activities

Make up a story about tarantulas. Be sure to include information from this book. Draw or paint pictures to illustrate your story.

Visit a zoo to see tarantulas and other arachnids. How are tarantulas similar to other kinds of arachnids in the zoo and how are they different?

Some people call both spiders and insects "bugs." Are these creatures the same? Go to the library and find out how spiders are similar to insects and how they are different.

Glossary

abdomen (AB-duh-muhn)—the back part of a tarantula's body

arachnids (uh-RACK-nidz)—members of a group of animals with eight legs. Spiders, ticks, and scorpions are arachnids.

arboreal (ar-BOR-ee-uhl)—living in trees

egg sac—the bag made of silk in which a spider lays her eggs

exoskeleton (ek-soh-SKEL-uh-tuhn)—the tarantula's hard, protective skin

fangs—long, pointed teeth

molting—getting rid of the old skin to make way for a new one

nocturnal—active at night

predators (PREH-duh-turz)—animals who hunt other animals for food

prey—animals who are hunted and eaten by other animals

prosoma (proh-SOH-muh)—the front part of a spider's body

spiderlings—baby spiders

venom—poison

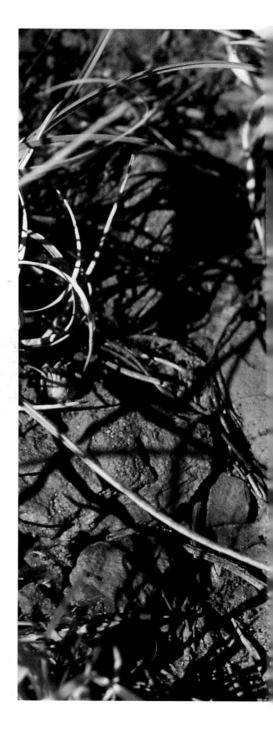

Index

Pages listed in **bold** type refer to photographs.

About the Author

Conrad J. Storad grew up in Barberton, Ohio, amidst rolling, wooded hills. He didn't see his first saguaro cactus, scorpion, or tarantula up close and personal until he attended graduate school at Arizona State University. Storad is the director of the Office of Research Publications at Arizona State University. His duties include editing and writing for the nationally award winning *ASU Research Magazine.* He is the author of several science books for children and young adults, including the Lerner Publications titles *Saguaro Cactus, Scorpions, Tarantulas,* and *AIDS: HIV Battles the Immune System.* He is a member of the National Association of Science Writers, the Society of Children's Book Writers and Illustrators, and the International Association of Business Communicators, and has served two terms as president of the University Research Magazine Association.

About the Photographer

Paula Jansen is a freelance photographer. She lives (and occasionally works) in Flagstaff, Arizona, with her husband, David, and children Ian and Hali. She is a member of the American Society of Media Photographers and has won national awards in photography from the Council for Advancement and Support of Education. She is thrilled to be involved in projects that promote in children both a love of reading and an interest in and appreciation of the natural world.